On Maudlin Pond

A Nature Journal
of observations and illustrations

by Mallory Pearce

ISBN: 978-1-7356192-7-9

Printed by IngramSpark, Inc., in the United States of America.

First printing, 2021.

Maudlin Pond Press
P.O. Box 53
Tybee Island, GA 31328

www.maudlinpond.com

In the Wilderness is the Preservation of the World.

Those words of Thoreau express how I have lived for much of my life.

I've always been attracted to nature: birds, wildlife, forests, wetlands, even insects and spiders. I've been an animator, illustrator, and teacher, but I've always been a field naturalist, making and recording observations and recording my notes and drawings into personal journals.

I believe that we need to experience natural wilderness for our emotional well-being. I've visited many ecosystems. I've enjoyed them all, but my first love are the marshes & forests of Coastal Georgia. This compilation is from my journals, collected for many years, from Tybee and Coastal Georgia.

Mallory Pearce

From the time when I was a child, I've loved birds and animals. Since I was a teenager, I beame interested in the big picture—the wildlife and the enviroment they live in. This passion began when I moved to Tybee and fell in love with the salt marshes and maritime forests.

I grew up reading (there was no TV when I was a kid). When I moved to Tybee, I wanted to know its natural history as one might know a book. I wanted to know the name of every bird I saw, to know the names of the flowers, the shrubs and the trees .... and to become conversant with the tides and seasons. In college I learned that there was a name for this passionate study of nature and its rythms: **Ecology**

Later when I matured I became more involved in political issues as they affect the welfare of people: issues of war and peace, justice, discrimination, affordable housing, etc, etc.

However whenever I saw a bird, a beautiful flower, a marsh, a woods or a large tree, I had to stop, to linger and look. My youthful passion reasserted itself.

SPRING

This journal is a compilation of nature observations during a year-actually many years. During a year in nature, the year begins in spring, the annual renewal. The deciduous plants, bare in winter, sprout new leaves. The annual flowers, gone in winter, sprout from the ground with colorful blooms. The evergreen trees and shrubs send forth new growth.

Birds which are silent in winter burst forth into song seeking mates to raise a family. Some of the singing birds have just returned from their southern winter haunts. The wintering birds have moulted into their spring finery ready to migrate north.

Feb 7   Sunny warm day
 A pair of Carolina Chickadees
have been clearing out a cavity
in a dead oak in our backyard—
bobbing in and out with sawdust
in their beaks. Aparently they
are preparing a cavity for a
nest to raise their young.
  They will nest in any place
with a cavity including a metal
pipe in our backyard.

4

Feb 23

Clouds covered the sky and gusts of wind came from the southwest. The clouds displayed monumental architecture. There were several layers of cumulus clouds. The lower layer displayed shades of blue & gray, but windows in this layer revealed towering columns of cumuli that reflected pink tints from the lowering sun. The clouds constantly sifted revealing a saturated band of orange. Then the western sky became vermillion blended with rose-red; the sky appeared ablaze with red. The sky darked to magenta pink and purple then darkened to dark gray as night descended.

Black Vulture

Two black vultures were standing
besides the road and I stopped to
sketch them. They were interested in
a squirrel carcass on the road; they
would walk to the carcass, pluck a
morsel then run back off the road to
avoid the oncoming cars. They walked
and ran with a long stride suggesting
their relatives, the storks.

White Ibis
Memorial Park

February – In northern climes spring begins in late March or April. In the subtropical climate of Tybee and other islands of the Low Country the first signs of spring happen in February.

Spring is proceeding. Cardinals, Redwing blackbirds and marsh wrens are singing. Many plants are forming new buds. The Vetches have unfurled new green leaves and blue violet flowers. The termini of the Slash pine bear tight clusters of small purple cones. Goldfinches still in winter garb feed on the seeds of dry stalks.

Feb. A Wind Storm

I awoke to the wailing of a Northeasterly wind. The stout oak and pine branches were bending and swaying as blades of grass bend in a breeze. The wind had pruned our forest. The ground was covered with lichen covered branches and twigs and yellow-brown palm fronds.

The gray ocean was rough and waves crashed against the beach with great force. It was raining and I had to lean forward to keep from being blown over by the wind.

Feb 20 -Great Horned Owls
   I was exploring one of the woods on
Tybee, I saw a large brown bird fly
on silent wings, then I heard distinctive
hoots: a Great Horned Owl. He was
perched in a tall pine tree. I heard
hoots from behind me; a second owl
flew to the same pine. They remained
there, hooting at each other from
different branches, looking at each
other but periodically looking my
way. Most of the time they sat bolt
upright — but sometimes they
moved forward to an horizontal
position. Obviously, I was observing
courship. I walked slowly towards
them, One flew immediately, the
other looked at me for several
moments before it flew.

Great
Horned
Owl

Horsepen Hammock

"ET"

Great
Horned
Owl

May . 4 2002

at Oatland Island -
The Eagle Lady

brought her raptors

Snowy Owl

This owl resides in the tundra
wilderness but on Tybee it perched
on the roofs of apartment buildings.

Feb 23 - Cedar Waxwings show up during
the migratory seasons : spring and fall.
They move in flocks through the tree
tops, uttering high-pitched "tseet" calls,
almost a lisping. Their favorite food
is fruit, especially ripe holly berries.

   This afternoon a flock of waxwings
were feeding on Yaupon holly berries
outside my window. They were in a
feeding frenzy, swirling around the
yaupon bush, bouncing off the
window. The flock of waxwings
moved into the oak canopy. Suddenly
a bird dropped to the ground from
the canopy. It was a Sharp-shinned
Hawk with a waxwing in its claws.
It flew into the brush, then dropped
to the ground again before flying off.
It was a heavy load; the hawk was
only slightly bigger than its prey.

Cedar Waxwing

Sharpshinned
Hawk

Redbreasted Merganser ♂

Horsepen Creek
at Camp Tybee

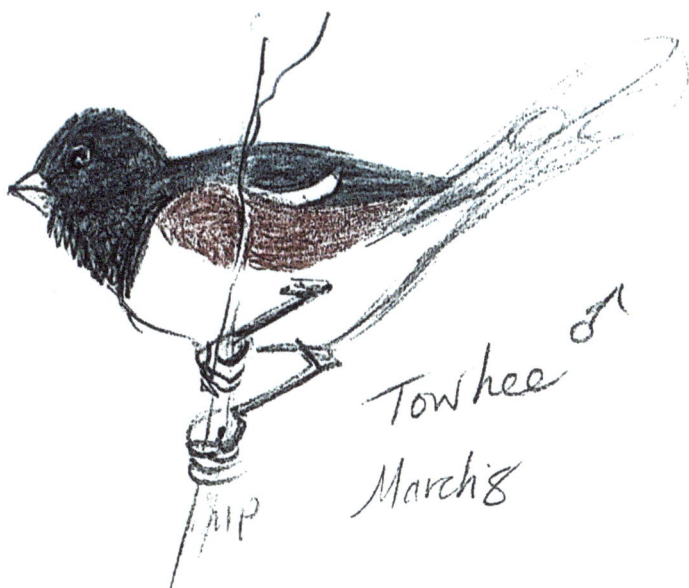

Towhee ♂
March 8

Mar 8 I hear an unusual cheep in
the bayberry shrubs — it seemed a
familiar call note but one I
hadn't heard for awhile. I
follow the call notes & spied a
male Rufous-sided Towhee. They
used to be very common on Tybee
but now I only see them ocassionally.
   The Song Sparrow was singing
from his perch adjacent to the
marsh___ .

March 10 The morning began mild with a gathering of clouds in the west. The rain came in the afternoon – a steady drizzling rain. Our coast is reawakening; Spring is coming. Cicadas are droning from the oaks. Monarch and yellow sulphur butterflies flutter about. The annoying Sand flies ("no-see-ums") are out in full force!

Bird songs are increasing and various: the whistling songs of cardinals, the flute-like triplet of the Carolina Wren, the slurred song of the Titmouse, the four-note song of the Chickadee and the elaborate song of the Mockingbirds, who have finally decided to join the spring chorus.

Fiddler crabs are coming out of their winter turpor; the males are waving to prospective mates.

March 11 – We were watching the sunset from a balcony overlooking the marsh. The sun dropped behind the distant pines, its color changing gradually from yellow to orange to vermillion. As the sun descended, it enlarged; the vermillion disc flickered through the network screen of pine boughs. Then suddenly it was gone, leaving a magenta after-glow against a darkening sky. Marsh-hens cackled in the dusk.

A thin fingernail trimming of a moon shone overhead in the now dark sky, but the tidal flow of the creek turned the reflection of the crisply shaped moon into shimmering jelly. Mullets lept, creating widening circles that disappeared when they met the dark columns of the marsh cordgrass.

March 14 The past few days have
been chilly with a westerly wind.
Despite the chill the sky has been
spectacularly blue with but a scattering
of clouds. Despite the chill, birds are
still singing.

Many flowers are now in bloom:
a vetch with blue flowers, a yellow
evening primrose ; white dewberry
(a blackberry) and the spectacular
Gallardia.

The sea oak stalks on the dunes
have been stripped nearly bare
with only a few seeds remaining.

Green dollarweeds (pennyworts)
cover the dunes.

March 22   **Spring**

The official day of the start of Spring was
Saturday, March 20; however Nature
operates on a continuum, the changes
occur gradually rather than "quantum
leaps," or a series of minute "quantum
leaps." We had a wind storm, a sort of
"quantum leap.", that blew over a few
trees and pruned many more. The yard
under our oaks was full of litter: palm
fronds and twigs and branches from
our oaks. The wind effectively pruned
our forest. A Red Cedar had been
knocked over and an oak tree was
now leaning into the tidal creek
that flowed nearby.

The mornings have been cold with
morning northeasterlies. Despite
the chill, spring is proceeding apace.

Flowers are in bloom: white
dewberry, purple vetch and redviolet
henbit.

April 2

A sunny unblemished blue-sky day—warming as the day proceeds. A morning of birdsong: brightly colored cardinals singing their liquid melodies from tall perches, the flute-like triplets of Carolina Wrens, the gurgling songs of Redwings, Pine Warblers trilling, the "wheeop" song of the Starling, the plaintives coos of Mourning Doves, the elaborate melifluous repetoire of Mockingbirds and Thrashers — joined by the cacaphonous repetoire of the grackles and the harsh calls and squeaky calls of jays.

The warm weather has returned after a week of windy cool weather.

April 2

The renewal that we call Spring continues. Young leaves are sprouting at the top of the sumac branches. The Virginia Creeper and Wisteria are now fully leaved but the Wisteria flowers are beginning to fade. The Toadflax flowers are rampant in every field but the time of the Henbit has passed. Spiderworts are blooming and will continue through the Summer. Many oaks are bearing tassels. The Laurel Oak have already dropped their leaves and are covered with a filagree of young leaves. Live oaks have not yet dropped their old leaves.

Parula and yellow-throated Warblers have returned.

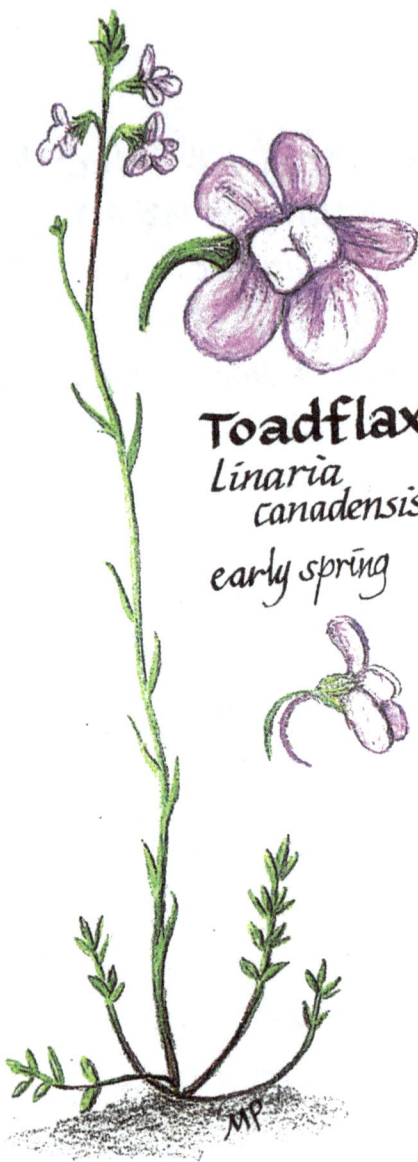

Toadflax
Linaria
canadensis

early spring

April 5
2008

MP

skullcap

Scutellaria integrifolia

early spring

square stems
(Mint family)

grows in moist soil

Camphorweed

Heterotheca
subaxillaris

seedhead

MP

Painted Leaf
or Wild Poinsettia
Euphorbia cyathophora

Spiderwort

Tradescantia virginiana

April 5   **Spring**

Last week was chilly, overcast and windy—
in the 40°s, but during the week, Spring
weather has returned. Today it's blue sky
sunny and warm—in the low 80°s.

  The Laurel oaks have already dropped
their leaves, which spiraled slowly to the
ground. Now the Laurel oaks are covered
with a filagree of tiny young leaves.
The leaves of the live oak are hanging on
a varigated pattern of dark green and
pale rust. The backyard forest is
active with birds: cardinals, house
finches, woodpeckers, brown thrashers,
chickadees and Carolina Wrens. The
jays and boattails are making a racket
but I heard plenty of metifluous songs:
mockingbirds, cardinals, the ascending
"tsee tsee" of ruby-crowned kinglets and
the buzzy trill of parula warblers.
Many yellowrumps are hustling and
blustling in the canopy,

Brown Thrasher
singing

April 13 – Another sunny warm day with
a cool breeze. A Brown Thrasher was
singing from atop a pine tree but I had
heard the mockingbird at our house
singing... albeit a more subdued form of
the song. Cardinals sing regularly,
Carolina Wrens ocassionally & the jays
regularly utter their squeaky hinge
mating call.

Parula
Warbler ♂

MP

On March 21, Lynn Hamilton gave me the
above bird, frozen. I painted/drew him
on May 2, 2022. Song: buzzy trill

May 3 – Hot, suny day. For the past
few days I've been hearing the great
crested fly catchers in my canopy ...
I'll be keeping watch to see if they use
the birdbox again. 1pm – a female
painted bunting appeared, eating millet
from feeder C. Observed a catbird.

Yellowthroat
april 29
feeding on
ground
in back yard

painted
Bunting
♂ singing
on oak branch

cardinal ♂
singing

Prothonotary
Warbler (2)

april 13
MP (in back
yard)

The yellowrump warblers are
still here & abundant, tsipping
continuously. A pair of cardinals
in the understory, are chirping.
A Redeyed vireo moves through
the canopy, continuously singing
his variable warbling song
Then I glimpsed a flash of
yelloworange in the treetops.
Focusing my binoculars I
saw a Prothonotary Warbler!!

Melodious birds sing madrigals

April 22 This morning the shadowy forest echoes with birdsong: the clear whistling of Cardinals, the variable warbles of Painted Buntings, the buzzy trills of Parula Warblers, the two-note glissando of the Titmouse, and the flutelike triplet of the Carolina Wren. The wren is small but its song is loud and resonant. The Mockingbird sings a long variable aria which can have up to a thousand individual fragments of song. Overlaying all of these euphonious sounds are the harsh cackles, squacks, whistles and wing flappings of the Boat-tailed Grackles.

The male Yellow-rumped Warblers are now dressed in their summer finery: dark blue coats, yellow and black-streaked vests and black masks ready to migrate to their northern homes.

April 24

The Season is fully underway; the days are now sunny and warm. All of the oaks are bearing new leaves. The sumacs are fully clothed in leaves and the bay and yaupon bear new green leaves contrasting with the mature dark green leaves. New shoots of briar and peppervine bear a reddish cast. The dewberry (a blackberry) has traded its white flowers for berries, most still red but some have matured into sweet black fruit. The dominant flowers are Spiderwort (a blue violet lily) and yellow Evening Primrose.

Ladies' Tresses are raising their helical stems. This flowers is an orchid; its small white flowers stick out at right angles in all directions from its coiled straight stalks.

The Marsh Hen

The marsh hen is the archtypical bird of the saltwater marsh, its primary home. Its call is a harsh, resonant cackling. Because of that sound, it's officially known as the Clapper Rail, however its vernacular name is Marsh Hen. Audubon called it the Salt-water Marsh Hen.

In the coastal salt marshes of the South East the marsh hen is abundant but it's rarely seen because it hides in the forest of cordgrass. However, its cackle often echoes over the marsh. One hen may cackle followed by another and before long the whole marsh echoes with marsh hen cackles. Sometimes they cackle at night during the full moon.

Sometimes when I'm quiet and still, I've seen them come out from the cord grass during low tide and walk along the mudbank at the edge of the water.

Marsh hen p.2

Marsh hens move slowly, lifting their feet high, stepping down carefully with toes spread wide to support themselves above the soft mud. Often I've seen them bathing. The bird ducks its head under the water then lifts its head rapidly, splashing water over its body as it ruffles its feathers. It continues the head bobbing and splashing repeatedly – then stops to preen itself. If the hen is startled, it rapidly escapes into the cordgrass. Once when I startled a marsh hen, it jumped under the water and swam to safety.

Sometimes the marsh hen eats small fish but its primary diet is invertebrates like snails and insects. The marsh hen is a prolific breeder producing five to twelve fuzzy black chicks twice each year.

Marsh hen p.3

Once I had an encounter with a mother marsh hen and her chicks. I was crossing a long walk that went over a mudflat. I noticed a marsh hen high-stepping over the mud. She was looking at me, moving slowly uttering a clicking sound. Usually these birds flee rapidly so I knew something was up. Suddenly a bevy of fuzzy black chicks burst from under the walkway running in all directions to hide in the marsh. The mother lept upon the walkway and charged me with head low and wings spread, defending her young. I backed away and left the courageous mother and her young in peace.

Grooming
marsh hen

MarshHen
chick

Clapper Rail
Marsh Hen

Moves head back & forth while walking

Mallory Pearce

The Painted Bunting

This is our most colorful bird. It resides in thick brush. This bird inhabits thickets of wax-myrtle behind the dunes. It's commonly found in the coastal regions.

The males sing a variable warble from the highest perch it can find. I've seen immature males, colored like a female, sing from a high perch. The males are aggressive; they fight fluttering their wings, butting their red breasts together.

It's a seedeater, eating small seeds, avoiding the larger sunflower seeds. I always enjoy seeing them at our feeders.

Painted Buntings & Wax Myrtle

May 1.
As the sun set, it was yellow-white as it approached the horizon. It went throught several shifts of color; the colors were reflected as a shimmering swathe by the tidal waters. The sun became orange-yellow. The sunflare disappeared and the disc appeared flat like a cutout. The disc became orange then vermillion and it enlarged (due to diffraction) as it sank to the horizon. The sky around the sun was a wash of salmon, pink, violet and blue. The sun became magenta as its intensity faded and it sank behind distant trees. As dusk was settling in, a green heron fly by.

May 1 - May Day

   Today was a very warm day - in the 80°'s.

   I have identified a resturning migrant that has taken up residence in our forest. The song was an irregular robin-like chirrupping. I glimpsed the bird moving through the oak branches: yellow-brown back, creme breast; eye stripes = a red-eyed vireo. The vireo's song has become part of the morning symphony, accompanied by the mockingbird, cardinal and Carolina wren. The chattering of o'erflying swifts is fairly constant.

May 4 **Night of the Full Moon**
The salmon colored moon arose above
the mists that lay along the eastern
horizon; the bottom was flat as if cut off
by a knife, then it rose above the clouds and
shone fat and round. As it cleared the mist the
moon cast a shimmering swathe of light
over the moving textured surface of the sea.
A dark Y shaped cloud, the only one in an
otherwise clear sky, moved in and
obscured the moon, save for a bright
white hole where it shone through
and a silvery edge on the dark cloud.
The swathe of light retreated until
there was only a sparkling patch on the
horizon. The cloud continued to move,
first obscuring the moon, then revealing
a pale yellow disc and a swathe of
dancing facets of light that stretched
from the horizon to the waves that
crashed on the beach.

May 6 Progeny

A pair of Brown Thrashers are raising
two youngsters in our backyard. The
young still have short tails and their
color is gray-brown not the russet
brown of the adults. The long-tailed
adults are always thrashing among the
oak leaf ground litter looking for food.
The young will hop up to adults in
begging position, wings ajar, beak
upward with open mouth. Usually the
adult will feed the young but sometimes
they fly to a new location to find food.
The young are still learning to fly.
They often fly to a tree trunk and
cling to the side of the tree.

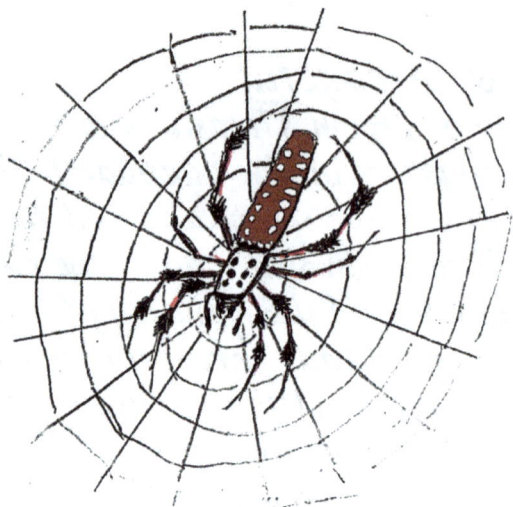

The Golden Silk Spider is colorful and large. The female is 3 inches; the male is much smaller. This spider is an orb-weaver and spins webs three to five feet wide.

They often spin webs across paths between trees. I have often walked into the webs and end up pulling off sticky strands of spider silk.

Cicadas

sing all summer:
a high-pitched
continous drone.
These are males

Adult Cicada
emerging from
Nymph stage

singing to attract mates. The nymphs
live in the ground for about 7 years.
Some species live underground for 13 years.
At the beginning of summer the nymphs
climb up trees and emerge as mature
adults. After years underground, the
cicadas enjoy a summer of hot sunshine.
The female lays her eggs on tree
branches. When the young hatch they
drop to the ground and enter the soil.
    The adults survive about a month.
After years in the dark, Cicadas
enjoy a glorious summer of Love.

May 12 *The Night Bird*

    The Chuck-Will's-Widow sits on her eggs with half-closed eyes. Her mottled black, brown and grey colorations blends with ground litter of russet oak leaves and pine needles. A pine cone lies next to her and that's how I find her.

    One wonders how her species survives at all. Her eggs lie on the ground exposed to predatory raccoons or the feet of humans passing by. The protective coloration and the fact that this frogmouth of a bird will sit unperturbed until the last moment are the secrets to its survival. This gargoyle bird will also move its eggs, probably in its large mouth.

    As long as we have forests, the loud whistling song, "Chuck-Will's-Widow" will echo all night, the night song of the South.

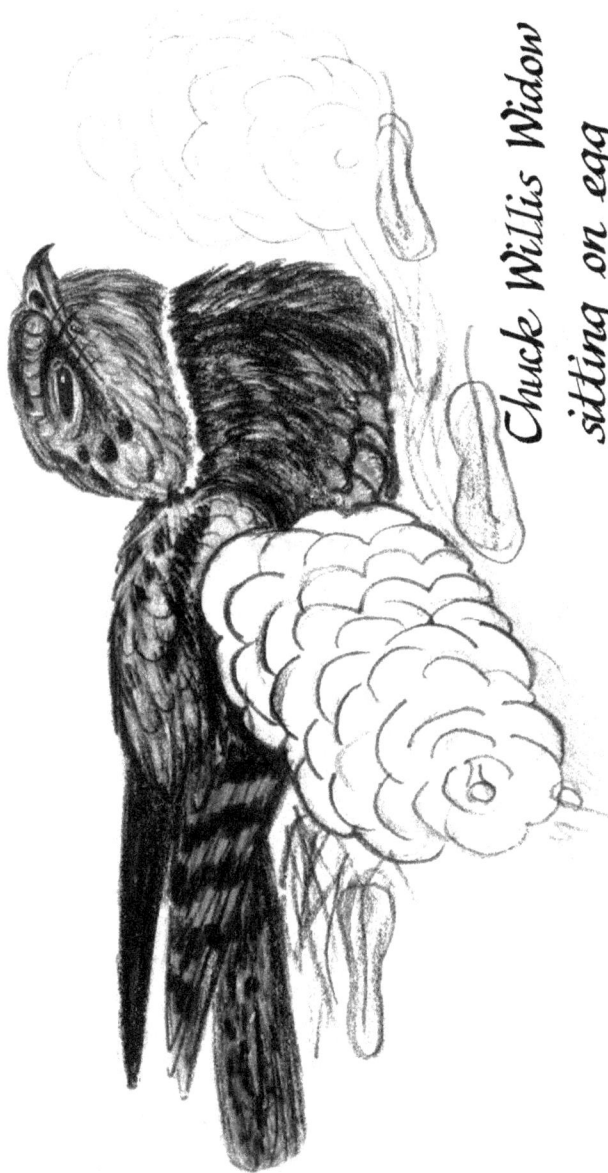

Chuck Willis Widow sitting on egg

May 30

The field across from our house is full of Ladies Tresses - the unique coiled orchid flowers with the blossoms arrayed around the stem helically. Skullcap persists; toadflax is gone, but the Spiderwort and Evening Primrose are abundant.

Birdsong fills the morning air - mating and establishing territory is underway. Green Herons are common in the marsh. This morning I heard marshhens uttering a distinct sound = a series of harsh "keks" not the usual cackling. Was this a mating call?

June 20

A hot, humid day with a slight intermittant breeze from the northwest. The clear blue sky had only a few wisps of high flying cirrus clouds. Birds are singing: cardinals, Carolina wrens and marsh wrens. Virginia Creeper is bearing clusters of minute cream flowers on a network of red stems. Some of these flowers have already developed into unripe green berries.

The Rattlebush is beginning to exchange its red-orange flowers for green pods that will ripen and dry out into "rattles" that give the bush its name.

Rattlebush
*Daubentonia
punicea*

June 20

A marsh wren sang from a stalk adjacent to its nest: dry brown blades interwoven with green blades at the tips of the cordgrass. The male marsh wren builds many nests to attract a mate! The female will choose one and finish its interior.

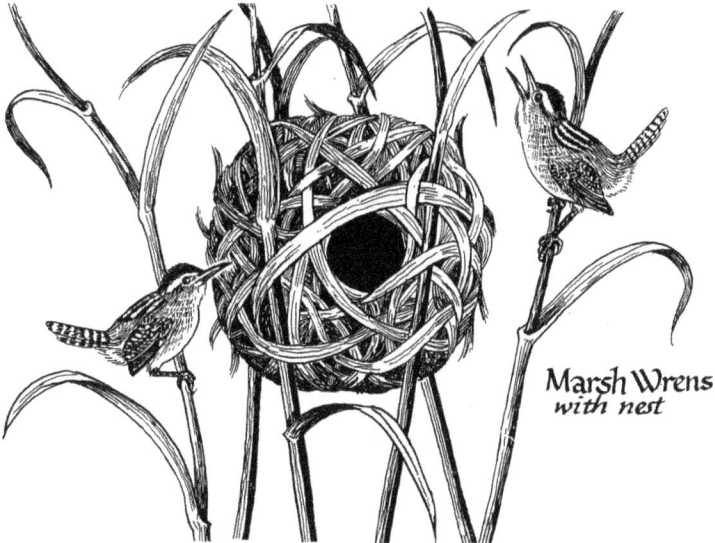

Marsh Wrens
with nest

June 2004 The Black Skimmer is a unique bird. Its lower bill is longer than the upper bill. It flies low over the water, skimming the water with it's long bill, looking or searching for fish. This year a flock of skimmers established a breeding colony among the dunes on Tybee's north beach. The nest is simply a hollow in the sand with spotted eggs - 3 to 5 per nest. When disturbed, the parents fake broken wings to lead you away. The parents fed their young small fish. Initially the chicks were downy fuzzballs with small beaks. By July they had left their nests and were running about but they still couldn't fly. By the end of July, the beaks had reached full size and the young had learned to fly.

Black Skimmer *with young*

half-grown skimmer

fledged juvenile

Green Herons

Most herons nest in colonies but Green Herons nest alone in the top of trees. They often nest in backyard oaks on Tybee. When they're old enough they leave their nest and climb about in the branches. They're good climbers but sometimes they fall to the ground. I took one in and raise it to adulthood; it had fallen from a nest in our backyard. Since that first one I have raised many fallen nestlings that people have brought me. Young herons eat regurgitated food that parents pump into open mouths.

I used catfood, pureed fish, which I fed into their open mouths with a plastic knife. Initially I had to pry open their beaks; thereafter they opened their beaks when they saw the food I fed them several times during the day. The young herons had imprinted on me! They grabbed at the food on the knife and even grabbed at my fingers. I was their mother! In some cases I raised them from a very young age-still with pin feathers. At other times they were older but still unable to fly. I raised several families - two to four each.

When they were old enough I put
bowls of live fish in the cage
and they learned to catch fish.
When they were ready to fly I
released them in the marsh
or my backyard pool. I
raised about 8 green herons to
adulthood. I know what it's
like to be a parent to young
Green Herons.

Green Herons
young

Young Green Heron
with pinfeathers
Wed. June 19, 2002

Young Green Heron
June 10
1995

Young Green Heron
at Pond

June 24   SUMMER

we are in the full throes of summer.
The marsh is quite green but the
dead stalks of last year's growth
remain. Sea ox-eye is in flower—
yellow daisies with a dark center.
The young barn swallows have
left their nest and and soaring
over the marsh. Its been hot
recently but today is overcast
with a slight breeze.

Cicadas are droning and
mockingbirds are singing.
The grackles are uttering their
repetoire of cacaphony.

My forest is lush and green
and vines are growing: Briar,
Virginia Creeper, Peppervine
and Wisteria.

A Helicopter trip

June 26 - On this day I had an incredible trip - a helicopter tour of the entire Georgia coast from Cumberland Island to Tybee, courtesy of the Georgia Dept of Natural Resources. Mike Harris of the Non-Game Wildlife Division took me along on one of their routine flights.

Most of the coast is wilderness. Tybee and St.Simons are the only islands with plenty of houses. I looked down on various tints and shades of blue, green and earth colors. When you look down at the water, the color is an olive tone with swirls and skeins of redbrown sediment.

When viewed at an angle, the water
reflects the blue sky but the blue is
often grayed and silvery - and where
the surf breaks there are long, sinewy
ribbons of white. The water forms
different patterns. The sea spreads
out in a textured sheet to the
eastern horizon. Near shore,
looking straight down, the water is
colored by sediment. Looking out
afar to the horizon, the water is
a shimmering pale blue with
scattered dark swirling patches
- schools of menheden.

At the bays and mouths of rivers
that go into the sea, tidal creeks
branch off and wind their way in
snakelike curves through the marsh.

The marsh itself is mostly light pea
green suffused with shades of beige
and brown. The high ground hammocks
are covered with dark green forests.
The forests themselves are oak or pine
or a mixture. The forest edges are
primarily redcedar and the tall
columnar cabbage palmettoes. The
redcedar and palmetto grow in
the pale green interdune meadows
along with dark green wax myrtle.
   On some beaches there were graveyard
forests, stark twisted whitened trees
killed by the encrouching sea. The
dead palms stood tall and bare like
rows of askew Greek columns. Tall
bare pine trees were held aloft
by an exposed network of roots.

We saw plenty of birds flying below the helicopter: pelicans, terns, gulls, vultures and an ocassional osprey. It's a unique view to look down on a flying bird. We also observed many seaturtle crawl tracks on many beaches.

Most of the Georgia coast is protected, a series of state preserves, National Wildlife Preserves and Cumberland Island National Seashore. The 'copter circled Tybee lighthouse and returned to the helipad on St Simon's Island.

The Georgia coast is one of the spectacular sceneries in the United States. On this day I had a wonderful birdeye view of this scenery.

Black Tern
(some mottled)

Least Terns _ by themselves widely spaced _ a few black terns with them.

Large congregation: Royal Terns, Sandwich Terns, Roseate Terns (black bill), Laughing Gulls (several plumages), Ringbill Gulls, Black Skimmers.

Royal Terns screaming constantly
High pitched bell_like whistle of Least Tern.
Many Least Tern calling (most are young)
Nasal barks _ Royal Terns.

Least Tern
young

Black Bellied Plover

oystercatcher

Greater Black-backed
Gull

Caspian Tern
larger than Royal Tern

Oystercatcher

Royal
Tern

Black
Skimm

Black Skimmer

immature

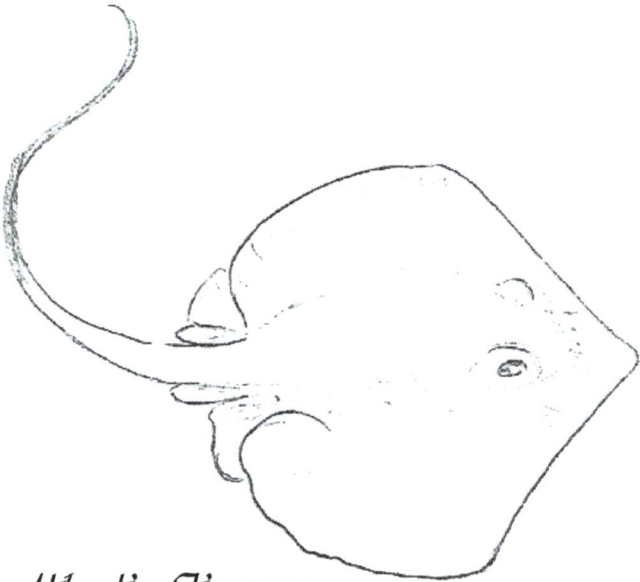

Atlantic Stingray

found dead on beach

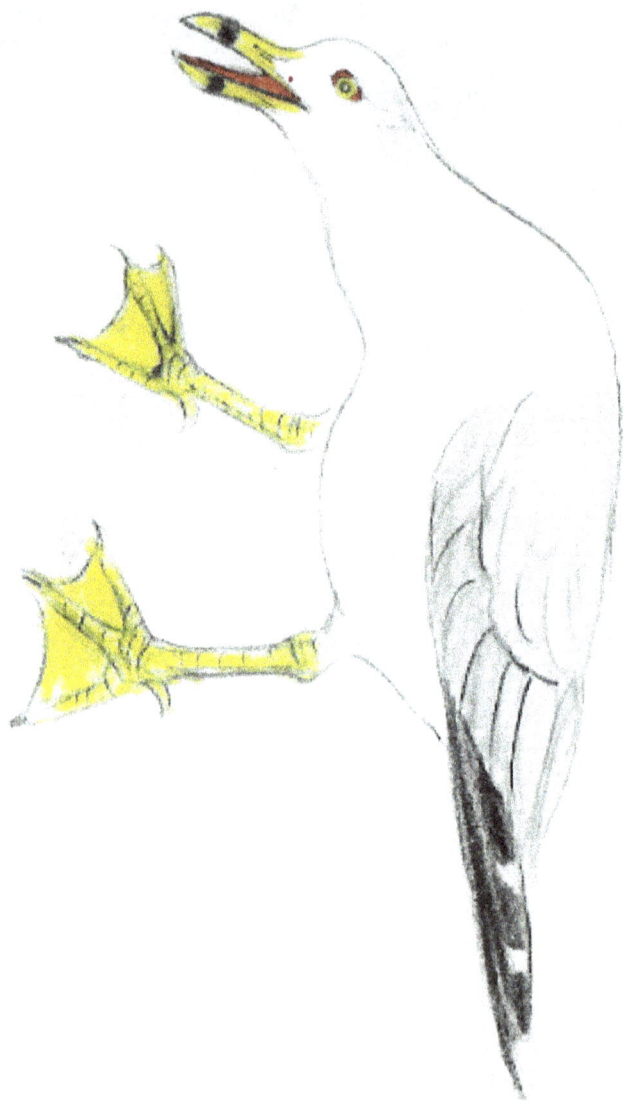

Ring–billed Gull

Detritus

The word detritus comes from the
Latin deterere which means to
wear away. To biologists the word
refers to decayed organic matter
especially plant matter that forms
the base of the food chain in any
ecosystem — the food for micro —
-organisms and small invertebrates
and fertilizer for plant growth.

In the salt marsh the main
source of detritus are the dead
stalks of the cordgrass, Spartina
alterniflora. The dead stalks
are stripped away by tidal
action. In the fall & winter,
the cordgrass turns golden,
then rust — and finally brown.

New green shoots come up in Spring.
It takes all summer for the tides
to strip away the brown stalks.
At the end of summer the marsh
is very green. The washed away
stalks form mats known as "wrack".
Some wrack ends up on beaches
where they are covered with sand
to form dunes. Most of the wrack
stays in the marsh and decays.
Fiddlers eat the fragments. Fiddler
crabs in turn are food for birds
and mammals. As it's broken
down further, detritus is food
for microorganisms. The
cordgrass detritus is a major
nutrient source for the richness
of life in a salt marsh.

stigma
anther

Marsh
Periwinkle

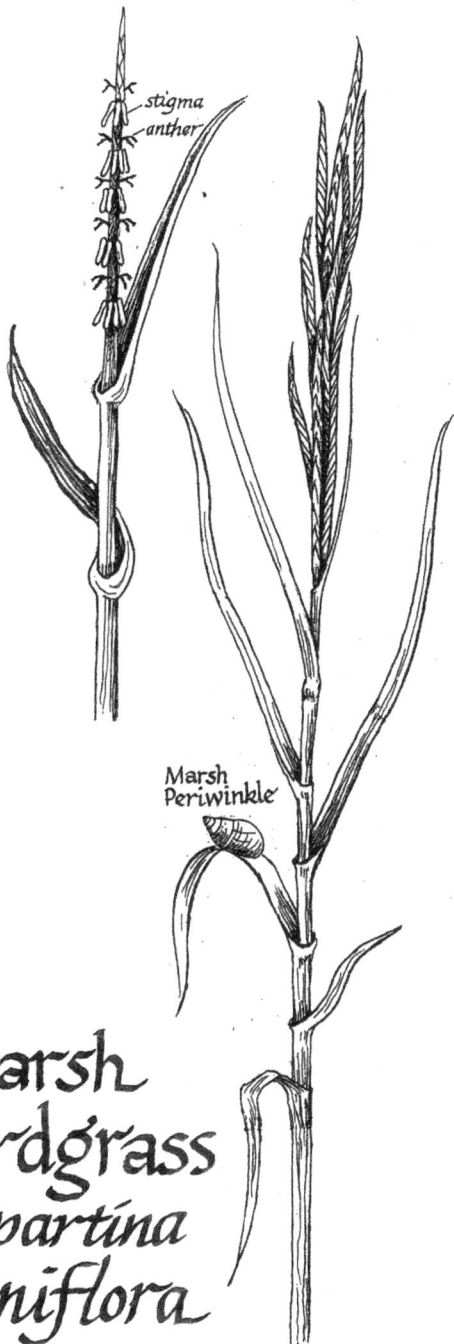

Marsh
Cordgrass
*Spartina
alterniflora*

Maudlin Pond

I had a shallow pond dug in the forest. Initially I put pond plants in the pond: water lily, pond lily, iris and pickerelweed. For many years these plants flourished but now the pond is full of leaves and the pond plants disappeared. I planted a four foot fetterbush by the pond. Now it towers over the pond. (8 feet).

I sit in my backyard to birdwatch. The resident birds are cardinals, Carolina Wrens, chickadees, titmice, thrashers and mockingbirds. Grackles and crows often visit. We are on the Atlantic flyway so migrants often stop on their journey.

It's peaceful, quiet and restful in my backyard forest.

White Waterlily
Nymphaea odorata
Maudlin Pond

SOUTHEAST

Live oak

Spanish moss

Sawtooth palmetto

EVERGREEN OAKS

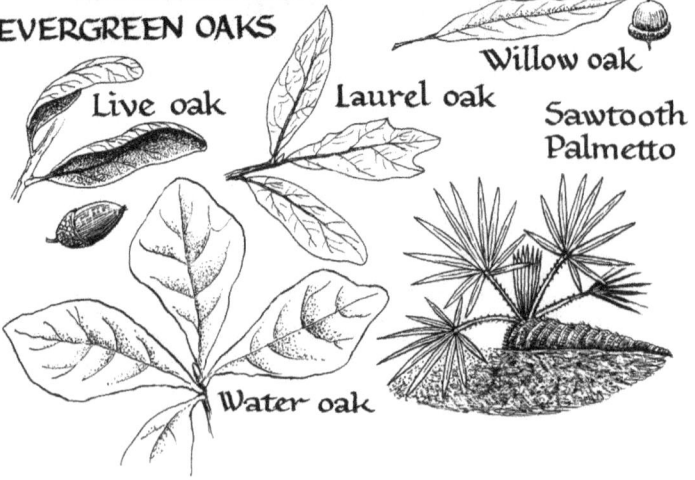

Live oak

Laurel oak

Willow oak

Sawtooth
Palmetto

Water oak

Backyard forest

When my parents bought our property in the 1950's it was full of shrubs. The shrubs were young trees and they grew into a forest of live oak (Quercus virginiana) and Laurel oak (Quercus hemispherica). We also have plenty of palms (Sabal palmetto). The canopy spreads out overhead; I love looking up at the twisted branches with their green foilage.

We also have understory shrubs: yaupon holly (Ilex vomitoria), Beautyberry and Laurel Cherry. We also have bay trees (Persea barbonia) and I often pick the leaves for cooking. Wax-myrtle (bayberry) is abundant.

We have a few Devilwood or wild olive (Osmanthus americana). Unfortunately we have an invansive plant, Russian olive (Eleagnus). Its berries are edible and birds spread it. All of these shrubs are evergreen but we have one deciduous shrub: Winged sumac. We have plenty of vines: the evergreen smilax (briar), Virginia creeper, poison ivy and grape. The most spectacular vine is Wisteria. In the spring clusters of blue flowers hang from the treetops. Many years I had a magnolia planted. It flourished and now there are volunteer magnolias all over the property.

Juniperus silicola

Redwing ♂

July 16: Everyday when I walk
along 6th St next to the Creek the male
Redwing Blackbird (sketched above),
follows me along the telephone line,
flying from spot to spot, calling and
eyeing me nervously. Clearly, he has a
nest in the vicinity that he's trying to
protect.

Swallos are about. I saw one dark
blue male, Purple Martin plus three
immature or female perched on a telephone
wire. Many Rough-winged Swallows were
sailing over the marsh.

Great
Crested
Flycatcher

MP

Fledgeling

Woodpeckers

The Red-bellied Woodpecker is the most common woodpecker on Tybee. When they inch up the tree, they hang on with their feet and brace themselves with their stiff tail. They also come to feeders. We also get visits from the small Downy Woodpecker, which can hang on a feed on small tree branches. The most spectacular woodpecker is the Pileated. They fly with a flap and a glide and their call is wild and pulsing. Once in a while they visit my backyard forest. I'm always thrilled to see them in my backyard.

Pileated
Woodpecker

MP

Most of the days have been hot and sunny (in the 90's). In the early evening of July 1, Peter and I took a walk along the beach from 6th St. to the jetty at the mouth of the Savannah River. Clouds were gathering and we could see distant bolts of lightning. A Japanese freighter was coming out of the river into the sea, moving at a good speed. Willets were scattered, feeding along the water's end. As we were coming back, it started to rain (lightly). That night, through the night, we had heavy rain and lots of thunder and lightning.

Downy
Woodpecker

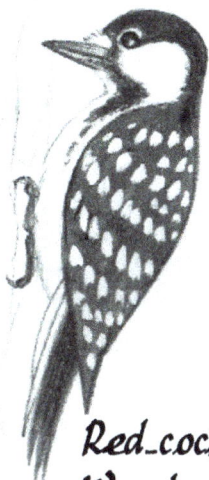

Red-cockaded
Woodpecker

Redbellied
Woodpecker

Herons

When I first moved to Tybee in 1950 I was captivated by the beautiful egrets and herons in the marsh. The next few pages have field drawings of various members of the heron family. We have 11 local species

The white egrets are conspicuous in the vast green marshes. The blue-gray Great Blue Heron is less conspicuous. The Great Blue and Great Egret stalk their prey slowly and deliberately. They strike their prey rapidly like a snake. I once saw a Great Blue Heron with a snake. The snake's head was in the heron's mouth but its long body was writhing and twisting as the heron flew with it.

Smaller herons often dash about for prey. I've seen Snowy Egrets running about in shallow water, wings spread.

Snowy Egret

Horsepen Creek
(Monaghan's dock)
July 14

Louisiana Heron, Horsepen Pond - July 9
3 Snowy's, 1 immature Gr Bl Heron

MP

Great Blue Heron
huddled against wind & rain
Horsepen Marsh · Jan 26, 1993

Great Egrets

Great Blue Heron on floating wrack
(extreme high tide) Sept. 26, 1990
Horsepen Creek

neck

Tuscan Red

Green Yellow

legs

Yellow bill

& eye

Tricolored Heron
Immature

Great Blue Heron

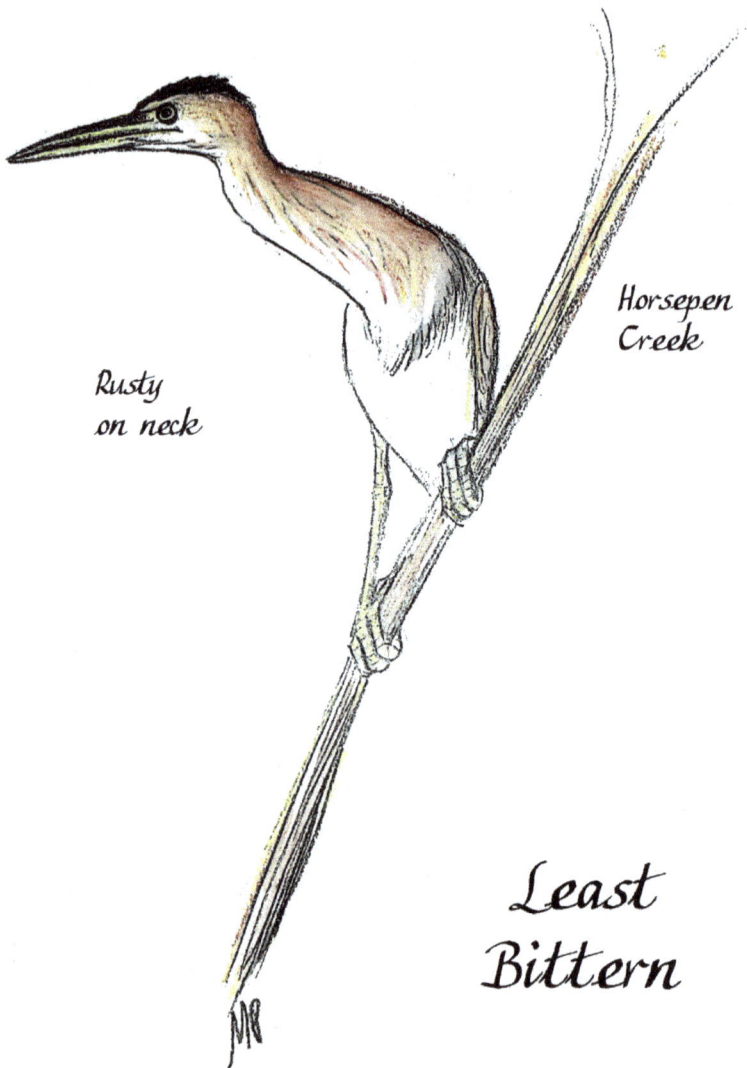

Rusty
on neck

Horsepen
Creek

Least
Bittern

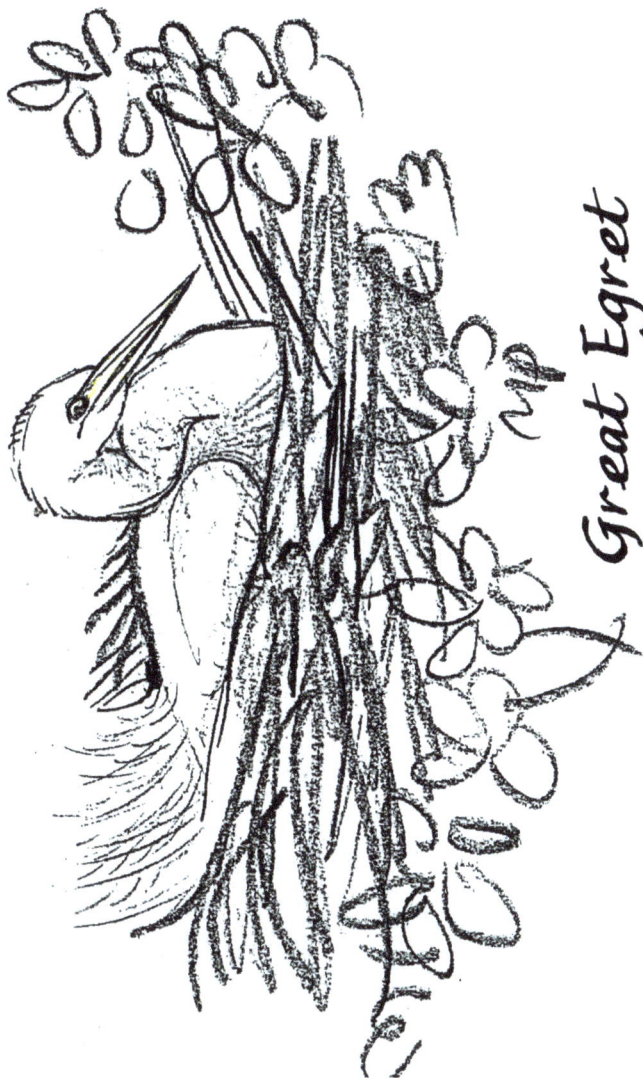

Great Egret
on nest

Great Egret

Snowy Egret

Horsepen Creek

The egrets had their beaks open
Because of the heat?

Yellow
Crowned
Night
Heron

Green Heron from Camp Tybee dock

The Wood Stork

The Wood Stork is one of my favorite
local birds. It's about 4 feet high, white
with black wingtips with a dark head
naked of feathers. Its bill is large.
When it feeds, it moves its open bill
back and forth in the water. When
the bill encounters a small fish or
crustacean, it automatically snaps
shut. Often the stork will stir the
water with foot to move the prey
within striking distance.

Storks are social birds. Herons
usually fish alone but storks fish
in groups—2 to 6, sometimes more.
Sometimes storks soar in groups.
I've observed as many as a dozen
storks circling together high in the
sky. Like vultures they don't move
their wings – their primary feathers
are spread out like fingers.

The Wood Stork

Storks and Herons nest in colonies:
a collection of nests atop trees, sometimes
hundreds of nests of great egrets, snowy
egrets, tricolored herons and night herons.
Great Blue Herons usually nest alone. The
parents take turns incubating and going
out to fish. When they feed their young
they regurgitate' partially digested fish
directly into the gaping mouths of the
young. Herons' nests are spaced beyond
the stabbing reach of their neighbors.
Unlike herons who feed their young by
mouth, storks regurgitate' the food
onto the bottom of the nest then the'
young gobble it up.

Unlike herons' nests, wood storks' nests
are next to each other, so that they look
like it's one big nest.

Wood Storks

Wood Stork
in Pine

Great
Egret
with young

Wood Storks
with young

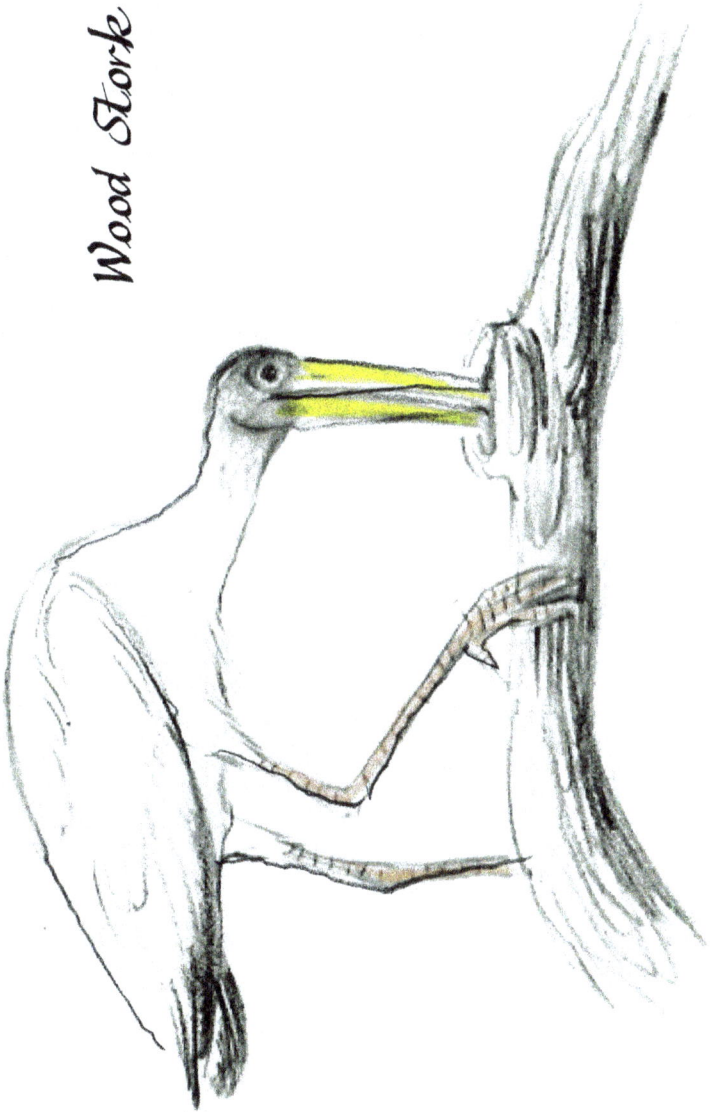

Wood Stork

Marsh Rabbit

Marshhen
Clapper Rail

July   Grackles

I sit quietly in the shade of the
oaks, trying to catch what breeze
filters through the foilage. A flock
of Boattail Gracles is visiting us.
A female is feeding a begging
young who is fluttering his wings.
The larger males ignore the
juvenile.

MP
July 8, 1993

Boattailed Grackle ♂
Wing flapping, wheezing
and cackling, fanning
of tail

July 8

We've are in a heat spell-temperature
in the 90's with little or no breeze. On
some days, the ocean is glassine smooth.
The only bird that has been singing is
the undauted Carolina Wren joined by
by the continous rasping sounds of
the Boattailed Grackles and the
drones of the cicadas.

In the heat of late summer few
birds sing. The mockingbird stops
singing - by early fall he may sing
short passages. The cardinal
ocassionally sings. Only the
Wrens- the Carolina and the Marsh
Wren — continue to Sing. The
Carolina Wren is the only bird
that sings throughout the year.

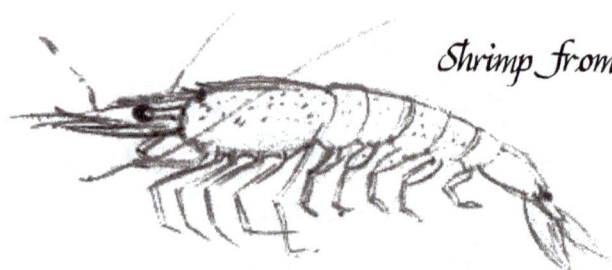

Shrimp from Tybee

Grackles posturing

July 8 - Thursday

Since the July 4th weekend, we've had a heat spell - temperatures in the high ninety's - with little or no breeze. On some days, the ocean has been glassine smooth. The only bird that has been singing has been the undaunted Carolina Wren joined by the nearly continuous rasping squacks of Boattail Grackles and the drones or pulses of Cicadas.

I've seen reptiles in the summer heat, usually in mid-morning: Green or brown anoles dashing among the foilage — one I saw a m-green male puff up his red throat. I saw a long slender Green Snake crossing a road — bright grass green on top, pale yellow underneath.

Common Nighthawk
on telephone wire
Ft. Scriven

at Horsepen Pond

40 to 45 Snowy Egrets some immature - no crests

6 or so Tricolor Herons - some brown necked immature

GrBl Heron at Horsepen Creek

Wilson's Plover
female or immature

July 10

The weather has been hot — but
the sky has been blue and the
air clear. The sea-oats on the sand
dunes are now bearing yellow-green
seeds. The marshes have became
green with only scattered patches
of dead stalks and lots of mats of
cordgrass wrack. The marshes
are in bands of colors: dark
green and tall along the creek
banks, the first to turn green.
Back from the creek edges,
the shorter grass is light
green. Next to the creek, the
grass grows taller because it
has plenty of nourishing
water.

Boattailed Grackles

These birds are abundant on the southeast coast. The male is black with highlights of blue, green and purple that shine when the bird stands in full sunshine. The male walks with a swagger; their long tail sways back and forth as they walk. The smaller female and immature are brown. Ironically the proud male loses its long tail during late summer moult and he has to wait for it to grow back.

Grackles are omnivorous and opportunistic, eating insects, small crabs, berries, fruit and even carrion. They also love human junk food: fries, chips, other leftovers. They gather at outdoor restaurants to search the vacant tables for leftover food. If you toss them food, they will gather and wait.

The boattailed grackle is a social bird,
sometimes gathering in unisex flocks.
The flocks are organised in a dominance
hierarchy, that is, a "peck order". I
have seen a pair of males squabbling,
wings flapping, feet entangled, together.
Most of the time the encounter is
non-violent, two males next to each
other, beaks pointed to the sky, flapping
their wings and making lots of noise.
The birds know which is the dominant
one. The grackles make an array of
sound: a staccato sequence of squacks,
a slurred ascending squeak, clipped
chips, accompanied by noisy wing
flapping and a fanning of their tails.
When courting, the males spread
their wings and bow to the female,
sometimes they fly after the female.
The boattail is a polygamous species.
The females nest in colonies guarded
by one or two males.

The females build their nests close together atop trees. The dominant male is in the center of the colony making noise; a second may be at the edge of the colony. DNA evidence indicates that the dominant male fathers most of the young, but the second male sneaks in and fathers some of them. The females build the nests and raise the young. All the males do is make a lot of noise. I once observed a male fleeing from a begging young.

The behaviour of the grackles, swaggering males and hard working mothers talking care of their children reminds me of some human behaviour.

The Boat-tailed Grackle is an intelligent fascinating bird to observe and study.

Mallory Pearce

Boattailed Grackle

July 13

Redwing Blackbirds and Marsh wrens were singing as I walked to the marsh. Redwings proclaiming their territory from high perches: High-stepping marsh hens walked on the exposed mud or slipped through the cord grass. The tide was low.

The sandy soil besides the creek was full of the hieroglyphics of animal tracks. Racoon tracks were common. Small round prints were those of mink. The larger round prints were otter.

Racoon

Mink   Otter

The Mink

Mink are common in our marshes but they're elusive and hard to see. One day in July many years ago (1952) I observed one playing. The mink came out of the water and began to bound in circles on the mud bank. He moved with an odd way of moving. Placing his weight on his forefeet, he doubled up his body and shifted his weight to his rear legs. Then he extendid his body and landed on his forefeet. He moved rapidly with a bounding motion.

July 15 - Thurs. A "Herp" day.

I went for a walk to Horsepen Creek at 10 am; the Cicadas were singing & a warm breeze was blowing from the west. This morning a few Redwings were singing, marshhens squacked (a drawn out sound) and the female Painted Bunting sang from the telephone wire. I saw the Snowy Egret fishing once again in the creek by the Monaghan dock; a pair of Green Herons took to flight, protesting vociferously. I saw a second pair of Green Herons from the Camp Tybee dock, also squawking & flying away.

Today was a day for "herps". I found a Leopard frog sitting in the middle of Sixth st and I picked it up — the frog made no attempt to flee. The frog was brown with a slight touch of green in front of its eyes. Its skin was moist but it was pretty far from water save for the saltmarsh (& the drainage ditch along 6th St). I sat down on the Monaghan dock to draw the frog, holding it in my open hand. Finally,

the frog decided to escape & left
onto the dock then continued
leaping until it disappeared into
the Sea Oxeye.

Near the Camp Tybee dock, a brown
lizard, probably the common Anole
rushed into hiding in the brush.

Continuing my walk, I startled a
sixlined racerunner, who glanced at
me then ran, living up to its name.

July 15

Leopard frog
sketch of frog —
but he escaped
beige with
brown splotches
Moist skin

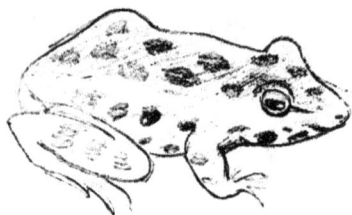

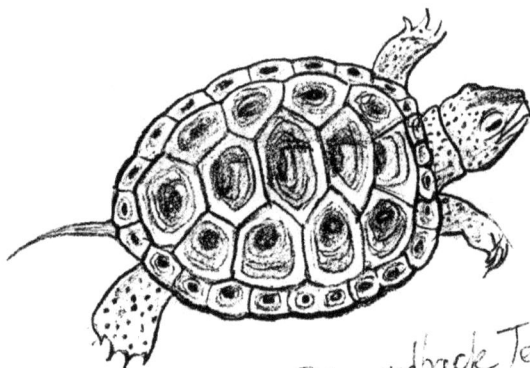

Diamondback Terrapin
at Camp Tybee
in touchtank

"Norman"

Southern Toad

Small Birds

We have many small birds that
hang out in our woods; some come
to our feeders. Some are year round
residents; others are migrants.
We are on the Atlantic Flyway so we
have visitors during the migratory
seasons.

Carolina Chickadees and Titmice
regularly come to our feeders. They
especially like the sunflower seeds
which they hammer open with their
small but stout beaks. They make
a variety of calls from the "chickadee"
call to songs during the mating
season. A pair of cardinals raises
a family each year in our woods.
The aggressive jays visit our feeder.

Small birds

Mourning Doves and Collared Doves feed on the ground on seeds spilled from the feeder. The Carolina Wrens is a regular. He sings year round. A Brown Thrasher pair raises young. They "thrash" on the ground looking for food. Mockingbirds sing at the edge of our woods, only ocassionally coming into the woods.

Many species of birds are migrants. The painted bunting, the parula and yellow-throated warbler are summer residents. In the winter the yellow-rumped warbler is abundant in our canopy uttering "tsip" calls. And we get ocassional transient visitors: redstart, rose-breasted grosbeak — and a Scarlet Tanager.

A Summer Storm

When we arrived at the Tybee Marina it was still sunny but the temperature was cooling down. As the evening progressed, a dark cloud began to build up on the western and southern horizon. At first it was uniform gray but as it rolled and billowed it took on a variety of shades – from a light to a dark gray. A cooling breeze was heading northeast, carrying the clouds with them. Lightning flashed in the distance. A series of large bolts connected the sky to the ground, worthy of Thor at his most aggressive. With each bolt of lighting, the crowd on the deck cheered and applauded.

The wind shifted to the north and picked up speed. The temperature dropped and Tybee Creek was — covered with small whitecaps. I contrast to the dark clouds, the marsh glowed yellow-green. The massive cloud rolled in rapidly overhead - seething, boiling, churning, billowing like a witches' cauldron - a constantly changing spectrum of grays-light to dark. Egrets, carried by the wind, soared overhead, white bodies contrasting with the dark clouds. The rain started with sprinkles, then the deluge came - heavy torrential rain. Then the torrent stopped and continued as a light rain.

We fed our cats
outside. A racoon
discovered the
catdish and
helped himself.
So I put out
3 catdishes –
2 for our 2 cats,
one for the racoon. We named
him Ben. One morning Julia, my
wife said, "Do you feed Ben?"
I looked out the window. Ben
was standing on his hind legs
staring at me. I went out
and put some food in his dish.
He moved away, then came to the
dish to eat .

One morning as I woke up, I said "Good Morning" to my wife. My wife said, "The racoons have had a good morning." She had observed them having sex on our roof.

The racoons raised their young in our attic. When they were old enough, the youngsters also ate in our catdishes.

Aug.8
     The weather is definately cooler
but the biting insects (masquitoes,
gnats) are around.
     The tree frogs were singing this
morning from a filled drainage
ditch. I caught glimpses of small
heads in the ditch before they
submerged. The nasal croaks of
squirrel (or rain) treefrogs echoed
from nearby thick brush.
     Mushrooms are flourishing.
I observed dragonflies and
butterflies: tiger swallowtails,
monarchs, skippers and sulphur
butterflies.

Squirrel
Tree
Frog

Green
Tree
Frog

Kingfisher

Aug 11

Camp Tybee

Aug 11

Kingfishers often perch on telephone wires, looking for fish in the water below.

A pair of kingfishers are protective of their territory, chasing away intruding kingfishers with loud rattling

Young Mockingbirds

Aug. 14

Two of these birds were in front of our house cheeping and squawking – opening their mouths to beg. The anxious parents hung about nearby.

Aug. 19 Starfish

Late this afternoon a wind arose,
coming from the northeast and gray
clouds covered the sky. The tide was
low but coming in — the beach was green
with algae. The edge of the surf was
strewn with Slender Sea Stars. Some
of the sea stars were alive, moving
their tube feet and ray arms. Others
were dead but still soft.

tube feet

Slender Sea Star

Roseate Spoonbill
Rosting with Wood Storks

Spoonbills often show up on Tybee in late summer. Usually in groups, usually they're young birds.

Sept 3

The sea oat seeds were ripe and
golden yet the blades at the base
were green. Boattail grackles
clung to the stalks to eat the ripe
seeds; one male grackle was in
moult and missing his tail.
The fiddleleaf morning glory
had extended its runners to the
maximum — a few had young
leaves at the end of its runners.
The white trumpet flowers
were open (this flower closes
at night). Before long these
bright green runners and
leaves will wither and die and
the roots will sit dormant until
new growth in spring.

Fiddleleaf
Morning Glory

Coastal Morning Glory

Ipomoea tricarpa

These morning glories are beginning to wither (and so are the Gerardia). They've been in bloom for almost a month; these vines cover the brush in various parts of Tybee Island.

Salicornia, Glasswort or Pickleweed
This plants grows in extensive
mats in the high marsh which
flood only in extreme high tides.

Sept 17

Jack Flannagan is the owner of the Crab Shack, a popular and successful restaurant on Tybee. The Crab Shack borders the Salt Marsh. Jack invited me to meet his tame otter, Otto. The otter lives wild in the marsh but he's lost his fear of man and will take fish from Jack's hand.

I was a few feet from the otter as Jack fed him a fish. Jack put on a heavy work glove. The otter grabbed the glove and began to tug and play as a puppy might. I made many sketches. I have never been this close to an otter. Other people came down to see the otter. The otter was unconcerned.

"Otto" otter
Chimney Creek, Sept. 17

147

Chimney Creek, Sept. 17

chimney creek, Sept. 17

MP

Sept 19   The tide was low, exposing
mudbanks. On one of these mudbanks
a green heron stalked. The Green
Heron stalks with body held low,
parallel to the ground or often tilted
forward, lifting his legs and setting
them down carefully. This bird was
moving slowly but I've seen them run.
   The bright morning sun created
sparkling facets in the blue-sky tidal
waters. But if you looked straight
down, the water was dark and muddy
with linear Arabesques of sediments.

This squirrel came
to our feeder.
He had a white
tipped tail. For
a couple of years
I observed a blond
squirrel in our backyard.
I've seen squirrels with tan or white
fur at scattered locations on Tybee.
Recessive genes may be expressed in
an isolated population; this is
known as "genetic drift". A
recessive gene such as tan or white
fur may be expressed in an
isolated small population as
may happen on an Island.

Grey Squirrel
in Oak Tree
at Mother's home

July 7
Carolina Wren
in shrubbery

(both of these
animals were
observed from our
living room window)

Gray
Squirrel

153

Gray Squirrel
(Sciurus carolinensis)

Often I sit outside and watch squirrels dashing through the treetops, often leaping through the air to another branch which may be very thin. They never fall. Their paws (hands) are able to grasp the rough bark of the tree branches. If they grab a smooth surface on a metal pipe, they slide. They are agile, graceful and fast. Once we had a cat who would chase them up a tree. By the time the cat reached the top of the tree, the squirrel was several trees away.

Oct. 2 — Beauty Berry (Callicarpa americana)
Verbenaceae (Verbena family) —
in fruit since August.

Beauty Berry
Callicarpa
americana

Oct 6 The Dunes in Autumn

The Sea Oat seeds are ripe and golden. The fiddleaf Morning glories are still green but flowers are gone. The Seaside Elders are always green but the seeds are dry, empty husks. The interdune meadows are full of flowers: camphorweed, goldenrod and yellow, orange and red Lantana. The latter two attract butterflies. We are in the midst of the butterfly migration, especially Gulf Fritillaries and Long-tailed Skippers. They gather at the flowers: a spectacle of color: butterflies and flowers.

Gulf Fritillary

Longtailed Skipper

panicle
of seeds

In the fall
the panicles
turn golden,
but the basal
leaves (blades)
are still green.

Uniola paniulata
Sea Oats – Oct 1

← blades are curled.

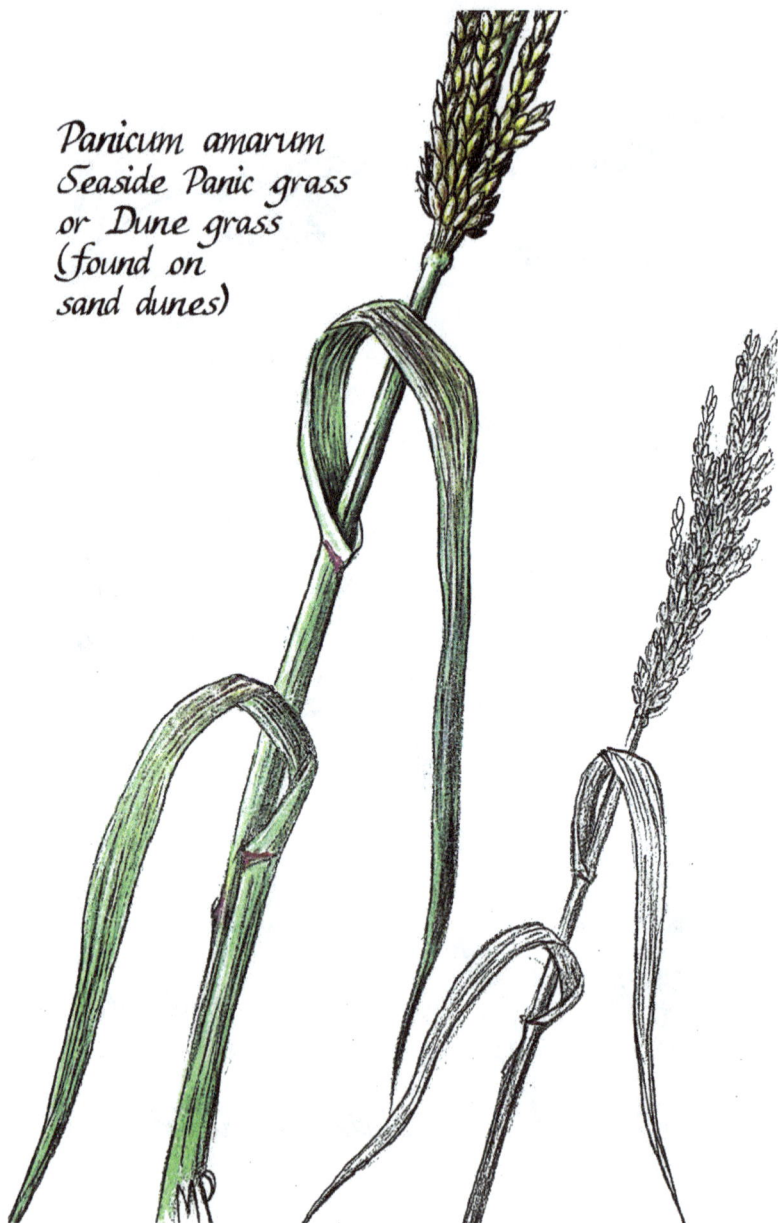

Panicum amarum
Seaside Panic grass
or Dune grass
(found on
sand dunes)

Coastal Dropgrass

Sporobolus indicus collected in the dunes and adjacent beaches on Oct. 1 — Ft. Scriver clusters of this grass, connected by runners, grew seaside of the seaoat-capped dune mounds.

In a marshy area near the beach, I identified the Bulrush.

Ghost Crab
lives in dunes

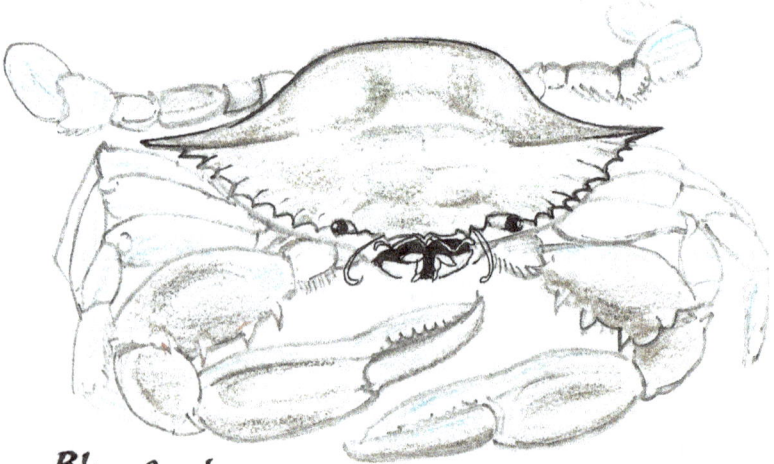

Blue Crab

Oct 15 A Sunset

The past few days have been sunny and mild
with blue skies, mostly clear but today small
cumulus clouds were scattered over the blue.
Despite the mild weather, fall is on its way.

Yesterday was a warm day but on the
horizon was a slight pink haze. The haze
created a spectacular sunset last night.
After the crimson disc descended below
the horizon, the haze diffused the light
into a spectrum: dark violet at the
horizon blending into magenta to red.
The tidal creek was glassy with a
scattering of ripples that reflected
the changing hues of orange, red and
magenta. The colors at the horizon
became even more intense before fading.

A Dolphin broke through the colorful
water, raising his tail high as he
descended.

Dolphins

♂ Yellowrump
Warbler

The most abundant bird in my woods is the
yellowrump warbler, the most common local
warbler during the late fall & winter months.
The yellowrumps are constantly on the move,
"tchipping" all the while, moving from the
topmost twigs of the oaks to the understory
shrubs to the tall water hyacinth stalks in my
pond, flying in swooping, twisting & even
fluttering, hovering flight mainly catching
small insects but occasionally stopping to
pluck a red berry from the yaupon shrubs.
"My" mockingbird & his neighbor have decided
to declare their property, both are singing.
The beautiful mockingbird songs are now joined
by the jays screams & squeaks & the squawks
& rasps of the boattail grackles.

Yellowrump
catching
insects on
the wing
Oct 31

Blackpoll
Warbler

Black & White Warbler

Yellow billed Cuckoo

Nov. 10 - We've had chilling Northeasterly wind for the past few days. Tonight was the night of the full moon and I walked to the beach about 10 p.m. to take a look. The Ocean was rolling and seething due to the strong force of the wind. The pale moon, its cratered face clearing showing, cast its spectral light over sea and dune and gave a slight blue tint to the sky. Layers of clouds, pale from the moonlight, lay along the horizon. Facets of moonlight danced over the rolling surface of the Sea.

I was standing among the dunes. Tall and dry sea oat stalks bowed gently before the wind. A beautiful and magical night!

The Cottonbush released its
parachuted seeds to the strong
wind. When the seeds are mature,
the Cottonbush or Groundsel Tree
looks like it's decorated with puffballs of white cotton candy. Most
of these bushes have been stripped
of their cotton by the wind
revealing the green of their
evergreen leaves. Before the
seeds disperse they are held tightly
by the bracts.

Then one day they open and the
gossamer parachutes take to the air.

Cottonbush or Tree
Groundsel
Bacchario
halimifolia

Hooded
Merganser

Cattle
Egret
in pinetree

Nov. 19   Fall

Sunny unblemished blue skies persist
but the chill has passed. The fiddler
crabs which had been hiding in their
burrows during the chill weather,
inch out of their hiding places to
enjoy the sun, ready to scurry back
into hiding if something startles them.
Gulf fritillaries, the only butterfly still
around, visit the remaining flowers.
Lantana shrubs still bear orange, red
and yellow flowers; Camphorweed
and Evening Primose still bear
yellow blooms but most flowers are
gone. The lush redviolet Beauty
Berries are turning black and its
leaves are yellowing. The sumac
leaves are scarlet and dropping
leaving russet seed clusters.

Nov. 19 Fall p.2

Five-fingered, wine-red Virginia
Creeper vines decorate trees and
brush, its red leaves contrasting
with the green of the evergreen
plants. The gossamer seeds of the
groundsel trees float, swirl and
dance in the breeze like a congregation
of minute fairies. The palm fronds
rattle and the pines sigh in the
breeze. The sound of the wind
in the pines can be described
as a result of air rushing through
rows of the pine needles creating
sound waves. To human ears,
it's a mournful sound as if the
pines were lamenting their
fate.

Nov. 20

An exciting, blustery, Northeasterly day. The strong wind created a symphony of sound: whistles, sighs, whispers and moans. Pines will sigh with even a slight breeze but today they were wailing mournfully. The stiff-leaved Palmettoes were rattling vigorously and even the usually silent oaks were sighing and whispering.

The gray ocean was rocking and rolling. The waves had deposited a thin line of foam on the beach. Ovoid rocks that looked solid but were made of soft mud were strewn over the beach.

The stiff sea oat stalks bowed with the wind

Nov 20 p.2

On the beach the wind was intense but in the marsh, the wind was only slightly modified by the intervening clusters of trees and shrubs.

The outgoing tides in the twisted pathway of the marsh creek were in some areas in synchrony with the force of the wind; in other areas the forces of tides and wind were contrary, resulting in complex and furrowed wave patterns moving in opposite directions.

Gulls soar like vultures. A Great Blue Heron took to flight; he glided on fixed wings, zigzagging to control his direction, settling down in a distant part of the creek.

Nov. 21

A Bald Eagle landed on a pole
beside the road that crosses the marsh.
Many years ago we had an eagle's nest
and the pair of eagles would fly over
Tybee.. Then they dissappeared!

In recent years they are returning
to Georgia and I see them from time
to time. I'm always thrilled when
I see an eagle!

Bald Eagle
Oatland Island

Eagle's nest - 1950   *Spanish Hammock, Tybee GA.*

Saturday, Dec. 11

A sunny blustery windy chilly day!
The wind is coming from the northwest
and is gusting up to 25 mph. The pines
are wailing. I heard the scream of a
Redtailed Hawk: two of these hawks
were soaring on the strong wind,
sometimes stationary as they faced
the wind, sometimes banking to
move ahead or twisting their tails
to reveal russet feathers. A turkey
vulture soared nearby but he
was being buffeted about like an
unsteady kite. This vulture is light
in weight in proportion to its wing
surface. They float on the air
bouncing in gusts of wind.

Pelicans

The Brown Pelican is the archtypical bird of the sea. It stays here year round and lines of pelicans are always flying just offshore. When you watch them in a line, one may flap then hold its wings fixed, then another and so on down the line. Flying in a line or V improves their aerodynamic efficiency.

Brown Pelicans dive for fish. No other species of pelican dives. The larger White Pelican, which shows up on the Georgia coast ocassionally, fishes while swimming, dipping its head under water to scoop up a fish.

The brown pelican also soars over the marsh, diving in the tidal creeks. They nest on isolated islands, surrounded by colonies of terns, skimmers & gulls.

Brown Pelican
at Horsepen Creek
at his usual post.

Brown Pelican
(total of 3)
at Camp Tybe Dock
(there were 6 earlier)

Jan 20 – The chilling Northeasterly
continues, it's always more intense at
the beach than inland where the trees
provide protective barrier. The velocity
this morning is 20mph whereas
yesterday afternoon it ranged
from 25 to 35 mph.

Scaup

Loon in Tybee Creek
observed from Marina

Bluebird ♂
at Horsepen
Pond

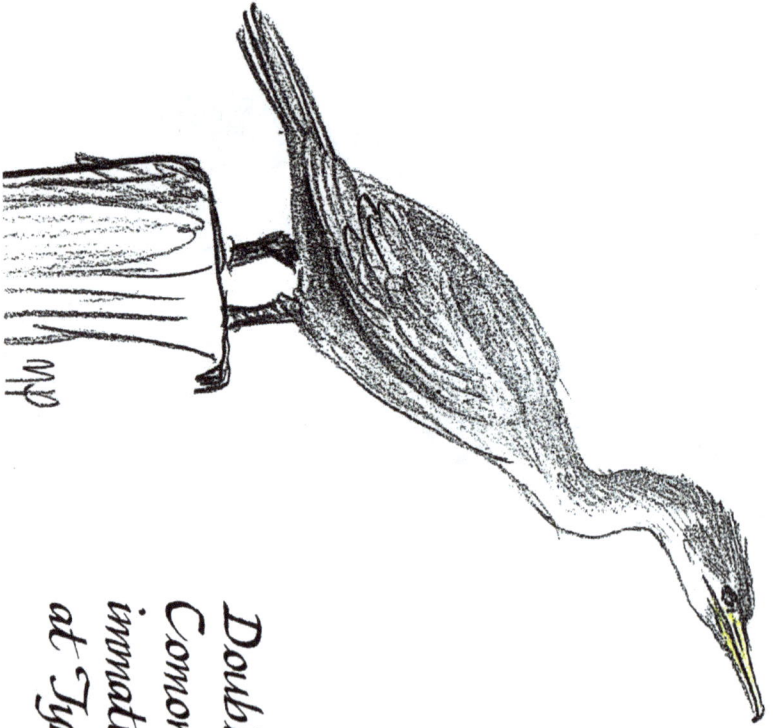

Double-crested
Comorant
immature
at Tybee Marina

Dec. 25 Christmas

Today is a sunny, relatively warm day—
blue skies with scattered cumuli puffballs,
but during the past week we've had
morning frost. Usually it warmed up by
midday.

The marsh is straw-colored. The tall
stalks have a few seeds clinging to them.
Young green blades appear at the bases
of the tall yellow cordgrass stalks. The
decidous trees are bereft of leaves but
the prickly ash (tooth-ache tree) has a
few young sprouts. The leafless Sumac
bears hanging clusters of maroon
berries. The evergreen bushes are
bearing fruit: yaupon holly-red
berries ; juniper and wax-myrtle-
blue-gray berries.

January **Gannets**

Gannets raise their young on rocky seaside cliffs on northern shores. In the winter they fly south. 100 to 200 gannets fly just off the shore at our island, Tybee. They rarely come to land. The ocean is peppered with widely spaced floating white bodies. The air above is full of circling, flapping, soaring and diving birds. The dive is spectacular: they fold their wings and dive at a sharp angle causing a large splash when they knife into the water. After the splash subsides, the bird floats on the water. After a moment the gannet takes to flight for another dive. Among the white adults are dark immatures. Dolphins are also feeding among the gannets; obviously there are many fish to feed upon. Pelicans, the Gannet's cousins, are also diving but their dive is more of a "drop" unlike the Gannet's power dive.

MP

drawn from skull

Gannets
from DeSoto

Great Egret
Jan 19
"windblown" perched in
a red cedar in Horsepen
March.

Jan 19. Tues. — Layer of clouds covered the
sky but it was mild weather with but a
slight breeze from the Northeast. Relatively
quiet day with background noise provided
by grackles. Two Carolina Wrens were
singing in response from our oak forest
joined by a buzzy trill from an unknown bird.

Jan - A small Bird Afternoon
   The activity of small birds in our back
yard forest was like shoppers at a mall.
A large flock of white-throated sparrows
hustled through brush. The wintering
sparrows were joined at the feeders by
other seedeaters: chickadees, titmice
and cardinals. The yellowrumped
warblers stay in the canopy above,
hopping from branch to branch or
flying from oak to oak, talking
constantly with quiet "tsips" A Yellowbellied Sapsucker (a winter resident)
was hanging upside down feeding on
Yaupon berries. Carolina Wrens were
particularly active this morning,
calling and singing – the males were
singing distinctly different songs.

Carolina chickadee

MP Jan 22

Yellowbellied
Sapsucker
feeding on
berries of
Yaupon Holly
(♀ or immature bird)

The warblers tend to stay in the
canopy above, hopping from branch to
branch or flying from oak to oak,
talking constantly with quiet "tsips".
Those that I identified with my
binoculars were yellow-rumped warblers,
our most abundant warbler, but it
pays to be observant because other
species associate with them___.

Great Blue Heron
huddled against wind & rain
Horsepen Marsh · Jan 26, 1973

Jan 26 The winds this morning were
especially strong and the pines were
wailing like tormented ghosts. Gulls
swooped by, only moving their wings
slightly to control their direction.
The streaked gray sky released a
steady drizzle of rain.
A Great Blue Heron huddled
against wind and rain, standing
in shallow water in the high reaches
of the high tide' rusty marsh. The
The Heron's windblown crest stood
erect like a showgirl's headdress.

Redtailed
Hawk

Solitary Vireo
Yellowrump
Gulls soaring

Redbreasted Merganser

Horsepen Creek
at Camp Tybee

eating large insect

Kestrel ♂

on Tybee 6th St
by Horsepen Creek

Barred
Owl

195

Cooper's Hawk
eating squirrel
in our back yard

YP

Bluegray Gnatcatcher

Whitethroated Sparrow

About 9:30 am – Tues. Jan 18
Whitethroated Sparrows feding on ground.
Chickadees and Titmise at window &
windowledge (with sunflower seeds).

These birds come in early part of morning.
Larger birds (jays, etc) come later – usually.

Horsepen
Pond

Ospery
(three)

Sanderings

Man, The Degenerate Animal

Last week, I was visiting and talking with several friends on the dock overlooking Tybee Creek and the wilderness of Little Tybee, across the creek.

One of my friends made the comment that man (humankind) is the only animal that needs to change his environment in order to survive. He went on to say that he felt no animal needs a house, pipes for water and sewage, heating in winter, air conditioning in winter, etc. In other words, from an evolutionary point of view, he postulated, man is a "degenerate animal."

Consider this, as well. Homo sapiens is also the only species that directly or indirectly causes the mass extinction of many other species, although there are specific cases such as cowbird versus Kirkland warrior.

My friend went on to declare that he has little concern for extinction since it has been going on throughout the history of the earth; it will take care of itself and will undoubtedly outlast mankind. On reflection, I decided that both of these statements are true, and are in fact, good insights.

I do feel that we must consider certain facts, though. In natural systems, as species become extinct, new species evolve and biodiversity is preserved. While the dinosaurs were dying off, mammals evolved. However, man-induced extinctions occur at a comparable rate. The extinction rate is especially accelerated because of habitat destruction. We are losing biodiversity and the genetic resources that this concept implies.

(Biodiversity is a current rallying cry among environmentalists.)

My friend is correct. The earth can restore its equilibrium; biodiversity can evolve once again. However, the restorative processes will take hundreds of thousands of years... or longer. The basic point of the environmental movement, I believe, is our survival. We may be the only species that is capable of bringing about its own destruction. Even if our species survives, the quality of life could be very degraded. Do we want to leave such a legacy to our descendants?

I left Los Angeles... with its smog, urban congestion, traffic, etc... because I prefer the quality of life on Tybee Island, a low key, relaxed lifestyle with lots of nature around: marshes, natural dunes, the ocean, maritime forests and lots of birds and other wildlife. The coast of Georgia is one of the few places in the United States where the original habitat still exists and to a large extent is protected. Although much ado is made of the destruction of the tropical rainforests in countries like Brazil (and the concern, I believe is proper), we, in the United States have already destroyed much of our natural habitat; at present there is a major effort to keep the remnant old growth forests (which are, incidentally, on federal lands) from being lumbered out of existence. (Jobs are an important issue but once those forests are clear-cut, the jobs will end!! We need long range thinking.) In California, more than 90% of the wetlands are gone. (In Georgia, we've lost less than 10% - most of our wetlands are saltmarsh... plus the Okefenokee Swamp).

A land without wetlands, without forests, without natural prairie and sand-duned beaches is impoverished.

Contemporary humankind needs artificial accoutrements to survive; we can no longer return to the simpler lifestyles of the Bambuti Pygmies or Amerindians who live in the tropical rainforests... nor should we even try. (Although these people and their way of life deserve protection).

Biologists argue that we need to preserve biodiversity so that we can protect genetic resources that can benefit agriculture, medicine, and other human uses. Ecosystem protection also benefits water resources, soil conservation, renewable resources such as wood, fisheries, etc.

All of this is true, but I argue that we need wilderness for our collective emotional and spiritual health... that we need to enjoy a vermillion sun setting over a green pristine marsh, to listen to a warbler or a thrush song echoing from the canopy of an old growth forest, to be enthralled at the power of ocean waves crashing on a natural beach with sand dunes and with twisted trees, to watch a brilliantly colored male painted bunting or a Redwing, with epaulets raised, singing from a perch overlooking his territory, to observe a while unobserved raccoon, a mink, or the elusive bobcat. As Thoreau put it:

"In the wilderness is the preservation of the world."